*a good writer possesses not only his own spirit
but also the spirit of his friends*

—*friedrich nietzsche*

How to Start, Join & Make the Most of a Writing Group

a quick guide for classrooms and writing groups

includes peer critique tips!

charity singleton craig

companion to The Art of the Essay

ts T. S. Poetry Press • New York

T. S. Poetry Press
Ossining, New York
Tspoetry.com

Cover image by L.L. Barkat

ISBN 978-1-943120-35-2

Craig, Charity Singleton

[Nonfiction/Writing]

How to Start, Join & Make the Most of a Writing Group: A Quick Guide for Classrooms and Writing Groups. Includes peer critique tips! Companion to *The Art of the Essay*

"How to Start, Join & Make the Most of a Writing Group" first appeared at *Tweetspeak Poetry* on June 5, 2015. This guide includes a modified reprint of the article.

"Peer Review & Critique Guidelines" is a modified excerpt from the 2019 T. S. Poetry Press book *The Art of the Essay: From Ordinary Life to Extraordinary Words*.

Contents

1

How to Start, Join & Make the Most of a Writing Group

The first time I joined a writing group, I didn't know any of the members, and since they didn't know me, I decided to write in a genre I don't normally work in. Not that I was "working" in any genre at the time. I had long since quit my job as a newspaper reporter, and not one of my query letters for nonfiction magazine articles had produced any assignments. What would it hurt to try my hand at fiction? I carefully crafted stories every two weeks before the group met, making enough copies for each person to read.

I joined a second writing group about the same time and continued with my fiction for this group, too, though one evening I read a short nonfiction essay about an eye-opening experience I had with a homeless woman in downtown Chicago. As with the other group, I handed out copies to each group member, and during the comment section, one man told me to be careful because I was clearly naive. I felt insulted, and tucked the essay away. I didn't change it, but I also never submitted the work for publication.

I moved away shortly after I joined those groups and didn't find my way into another writing group until about ten years later. By that time, I was working as a writer, and the input and feedback I was looking for was much different than my "naive" younger self.

Why You Should Be in a Writing Group

The writing life can be a lonely life if we don't find some way to connect with others pursuing the same passion. Perhaps you've heard friends talk about their wonderful experiences being part of a writers group. Or maybe, like me, you were in a writing group once but circumstances changed and you stopped going. On the other hand, you might have heard horror stories of writers groups gone bad and are fearful of making the leap. It's possible you are even in a writing group already, and it just isn't working out.

Writing groups aren't for everyone, but writing groups aren't all alike either. They come in different sizes, they have a variety of purposes, they meet according to various schedules. The first step towards having a good experience in a writing group is to determine why you want to be in one. Ask yourself these questions:

- Do I crave professional connection?

- Do I need encouragement?

- Do I want to encourage other writers?

- Am I looking for ways to grow as a writer?

• Would I like feedback on my work?

Writing groups can provide these benefits and more. Once you recognize what you are looking for in a writing group, the next step is finding one that can meet your expectations.

Joining an Existing Writing Group

The writing group I currently belong to meets at a café one evening a month. The women in my group (mine happens to be all women, but of course other groups have men and women or just men, too) have all become friends, and we share many things in common in addition to our love of writing. There's only one problem. The group meets about an hour from my home. Right now, I'm committed to making the two-hour roundtrip drive each month. But sometimes, I wonder if a writing group closer to home would be better. However, I don't know if there's an organized writing group I could join in my city. Maybe your circumstances are similar.

If you're considering being part of a writing group, step one is to determine if one already exists in your city or area. How do you find existing writing groups? There are several places to start. First, contact your local library. That's how I found my first writing group. You also can look on the community information boards at local coffee shops and bookstores. (You know how much writers like to drink coffee and read!) If you don't find a group using those resources, take your efforts online. Do an Internet search for "writing groups in YOUR CITY" or check Meetup, whose tagline is "Find

Your People." A few writing groups in cities near mine post their meetings there.

If you do find a group, the next step is to determine whether this group is even an option for you. Practically speaking, does the group meet at a time and place you can attend? Also, does the group allow new members?

If yes, then beyond just the when and where, here are a few other things to ask when you're considering joining a writing group:

• Who comprises the group—writers of a specific genre, geography, age, etc.?

• Why does the group exist? What is its purpose?

• How are the meetings conducted? How are new members introduced to the group?

• What does the group do during meetings—critique each other's work, write to prompts, listen to speakers, read a book and respond? Does the group do other activities in addition to their regular meetings (attend conferences, host workshops, create collaborative books or magazines)?

• Are there dues or other requirements for joining?

Once you find a group that fits your schedule and your goals, contact them to schedule a visit. Attend the group once or twice (if allowed) before you commit to joining. This will give you and the group a trial run together.

But what if you've searched and searched and can't find a writing group to join?

Consider Starting a New Writing Group

Maybe it's time for you to start a new writing group in your area. Where do you start? Use the same process you did above for finding a group, only this time, you are free to answer the questions however you like. Or, find one or two other writers in your area (go back to the library, coffee shops, and bookstores, or start your own Meetup group if you don't already know other writers) and together work through the questions above.

Planning from the start how to adapt your group to growth and change will help ensure a long life for your new group. Depending on your goals, you may want to organize the group more officially by establishing membership documents, setting up your group legally as a non-profit organization, or electing leaders.

Now What?

Whether you've joined an existing group or established a new one of your own, your writing group is counting on you for its success—well, you and all the other members. But still, here are a few things that you can do to make the most out of your writing group experience:

Step Up. Whether you're the founding member or are joining an established group, offer your suggestions for making the group a meaningful experience for all. Suggest activities for group meetings, offer ideas for group outings, invite potential new members if your group is open. Does your group need a Facebook or Meetup page to help everyone stay in touch? Could you be the one to create it? If things aren't going well, maybe you need to be the one to suggest changes, wade through misunderstandings, or offer a new plan for structuring your meetings. Sure, you could wait around for someone else to recognize and solve the problem, or you could be the one to offer a solution.

Step Out. Trust is built over time as members of the group get to know each other. Be the person who sets the tone for honesty and authenticity. Share successes and failures with the group. Be willing to kindly speak up when you have a different opinion than others. And if appropriate, let others in the group know when you're struggling personally, especially if it affects your attendance or your writing.

Step Aside. Although you may be an instrument for change or direction, a writing group can't be about one person. That's called a fan club. Lead the way, then let others take ownership. Encourage everyone in the group to participate in conversations as well as group projects or outings. When appropriate, delegate.

Step Away. Groups take time to operate successfully. Yours won't meet every one of your expectations at the first meeting. But if the members of your writing group aren't gelling or if your expectations are never met—despite your own best effort over time—or if other members seem to lack commitment, there may come a time to leave the group. Don't leave at the first sign of trouble. Every group will have its ups and downs. But if you've given it time and effort, don't feel you have to stay in a group that's going nowhere. Maybe it's just time for something new.

Writing groups aren't for everyone, but finding the right group for you will go a long way in helping you live a satisfying and productive writing life.

2

Peer Review & Critique Guidelines

As you practice techniques and write, don't overlook or underestimate the importance of receiving feedback on your work.

But first, an acknowledgement. It's true we've all been disappointed or even paralyzed by a stinging critique too early in the process. Sometimes, we've received conflicting advice from two different readers. And occasionally, we just disagree with the opinions of others but feel forced to make changes we don't want to make.

This guide won't necessarily make that all go away. But what I hope to do is give you some strategies for getting (and giving) better feedback on your (and others') writing.

Ask For What You Need

Borrowing from the National Writing Project's Guidelines for Response Groups, let's think about giving and receiving feedback on three levels. Rather than handing your writing off blindly for a critique or peer review, instead, ask for what you want or need at this stage of your writing. Do you want the reader to admire, inquire, and/or perspire?

ADMIRE: Feeling uncertain about the way your piece is coming together, or trying to find the aspect of your work that really resonates? Ask readers for only what they admire, inviting them to comment on what's working well. Sure, it has some problems. It's still an early draft. Make it clear to your readers that you understand that; otherwise, the more detail-oriented among them might not be able to let go of those comma splices or changing points of view. But when you just need to know which parts are on the right track, ask for only what's going well, for what they *admire* in your essay.

INQUIRE: When your draft is a little further along, or maybe you're feeling good about the work, invite readers to address just one or two overarching concerns they see. Of course they should also comment on what's working well. No one should ever turn down a chance to be admired. But when you're getting closer to "feeling" finished, having a reader inquire about a specific issue will help with what otherwise might be a blind spot for you.

PERSPIRE: Finally, before you send your work to a publication, invite a trusted reader, who also happens to know about grammar and punctuation, to go all out on your essay. Sure, they can tell you what's working, but more than that, you want to know anything that's *not* working. A trusted reader is key here, because now is not the time for tiptoeing around any major issues. You need someone who's willing to do the necessary hard work, to sweat it out with you. You're about to send this to an editor, and you'll want to put your best work out there every time.

Higher and Lower Order Concerns

Beyond giving yourself permission to ask for the level of feedback you want, it's also important for you—and any potential peer reviewers—to have a good sense of what issues to address and when. (You can include a brief explanation of the following along with any potential requests for review.)

The writing process includes two levels of concerns: higher order concerns and lower order concerns.

Higher order concerns address larger, "big picture" issues of the work as a whole—things like thesis or theme, purpose, structure, and development. Working towards a well-written piece means strengthening the work in these areas first.

After the higher order concerns are addressed, writers can work more at the paragraph, sentence, and word level, and other lower order concerns: grammar, punctuation, usage, word choice, spelling, etc.

Don't let the words *higher* and *lower* imply too much a sense of greater and lesser importance here. Both levels matter to your writing, and problems in either can spell trouble. Generally, *higher* and *lower* refer to the order of priority in which these levels are addressed. First, address the big picture issues, then the lower order concerns, since there's no need to labor over a comma in the introduction if the whole thing needs to be written with a different focus anyway. But for many writers, the writing process—from drafting to revision—will move back and forth between the two.

So, within the "admire, inquire, perspire" framework we talked about above, you may want to ask for admiration or inquiry mostly about higher order concerns. When it comes time to perspire, however, both higher and lower order concerns should be on the table.

Additional Guidelines for Group Critique Sessions

If you're forming a writing critique group, you might consider these additional guidelines as a format for your meeting.

Before You Meet

The person whose work is being evaluated should send a copy to each participant a few days before the meeting and tell the readers what they are looking for: admire, inquire, or perspire? And higher order concerns, lower order concerns, or both?

Each participant should read each review piece ahead of time and make notes about the work on the printed copy so the writer can go back and review them later.

The goal is to provide insight that the author can't discern on her own. Comment on what aspects you really like and why, and how the piece affects you as a reader. Be specific. Unless the author has asked for it, remember not to focus on grammar or spelling.

During the Critique Group

The writer whose work is being evaluated will read a short excerpt (250-300 words) aloud to get everyone engaged with the piece. This will be extremely scary for some, but it also helps us practice hearing our work the way others hear it.

After the writer reads the excerpt, she should remain silent through the comments and responses—a response sometimes referred to as "wearing the cone of silence." (I've even seen groups mime the action of placing a cone over oneself as each member takes a turn at being critiqued—though maybe your group would prefer to don a silent superhero cloak!) No matter how much she wants to explain or agree or clarify, the writer should just receive what's expressed. After each reviewer has offered comments, the writer should simply say, "Thank you." When the critique session has ended, the writer can send an email to ask for clarification, but for now, she should just listen.

Each reviewer should share a few of their more noteworthy comments aloud for the whole group to hear. When speaking to the writer, keep in mind a few guidelines to help ease the sting that criticism often brings:

• Comment on both positive and negative aspects of the work, even if the writer has asked for feedback that goes beyond Admiration.

• Begin suggestions and observations with "I notice" instead of "you always" or other phrases that might make the writer feel on the spot.

• Refer to the writer as "the writer" or the narrator as "the narrator" rather than "you."

- After everyone has had a chance to share a few comments, give the writer the printed version of each critique and move on to the next piece for review.

Having your work reviewed and critiqued can be painful. Plan on feeling a little sting even if it's not your first critique and even if the majority of the comments are positive. You may find it difficult not to respond to the comments during the critique session, but taking that option off the table will actually put less pressure on you to respond in any particular way. The important thing to remember is you are the writer; you can accept or reject any of the comments or suggestions. Try "in the margin" exercises when the solution isn't immediately obvious. (Note: "in the margin" exercises are discussed at greater length in *The Art of the Essay.*) At the very least, consider whether you can enhance or make clearer any of the sections that were commented upon. The reviewer likely has stumbled on a problem area, even if their suggestions for correcting it don't feel quite right to you.

Just like being a good writer, learning to be a good reviewer takes practice. Try to push beyond simple phrases like "I like it" and "It's good." Trust your instincts as a reader, and really work at providing helpful comments to your fellow writers. But also give yourself a break. If this process feels awkward and uncomfortable at first, you're likely not alone.

Inspiration & Tools for Your Writing Group

The Art of the Essay: From Ordinary Life to Extraordinary Words,
by Charity Singleton Craig

On Being a Writer: 12 Simple Habits for a Writing Life That Lasts,
by Ann Kroeker & Charity Singleton Craig

Rumors of Water: Thoughts on Creativity & Writing, by L.L. Barkat

Twirl: My Life With Stories, Writing & Clothes, by Callie Feyen

Credits & Sources

Meetup is a service used to organize online groups that host in-person events for people with similar interests. Meetup was founded in 2002 by CEO Scott Heiferman and four co-founders. The company was acquired by WeWork in 2017.

The National Writing Project is a network of sites anchored at colleges and universities and serving teachers across disciplines and at all levels, early childhood through university.

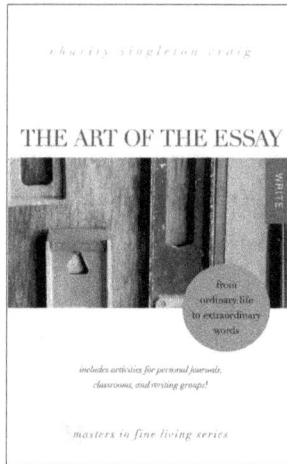

The Art of the Essay: From Ordinary Life to Extraordinary Words

What kind of writer are *you?* asks Charity Singleton Craig, as she opens you to a journey of discovery about the art of essay writing that explores both practical and reason-for-writing concerns.

From a near hummingbird disaster to a secret foray into hilarity, you'll find yourself inspired alongside the author—to reimagine the simple stuff of your life as a starting point for thoughtful, sometimes amusing, always voice-infused writing that's your very own ... as well as being a true gift to the world.

A great title for personal writing journeys, classrooms, and writers groups.

www.ingramcontent.com/pod-product-compliance
Lightning Source LLC
Chambersburg PA
CBHW030013040426
42337CB00012BA/760